Make It Fizz

A Guide to Making Bathtub

By Holly Port

HANDCRAFTED *all Natural* BODY TREATS

Make It Fizz: A Guide to Making Bathtub Treats
by Holly Port

ISBN-13: 978-0692202883 (Holly Port)
ISBN-10: 0692202889

Notice of Rights

Notice of Liability

Legal Disclaimer

Copyright

This book is dedicated to my dad.
I miss you every day.

A special thanks to

The Handcrafted Soap & Cosmetic Guild

for their leadership, promotion and support of the handcrafted soap and cosmetic industry.

Without their endless research and guidance to negotiate the rules, regulations, and best practices in this industry, we would not be where we are today.

Thank you.

"What soap is to the body, laughter is to the soul"
~ Yiddish proverb

Contents

Introduction

More than **seven years ago** I began this journey with a meager idea of making some Christmas gifts for my friends and family. The family and I were out shopping after my son had won the annual **Yule Log hunt**. Little did I know, stopping at a little boutique, that my life would be changed forever. I looked down and saw a lotion bar on the way out of the shop; and this is how it started. For one, I have always loved body products, but have sensitive skin. Your run-of-the-mill bubble baths were wreaking havoc on my skin. I knew I needed to make something that was relaxing and moisturizing to my skin **without any harsh chemicals**. After mastering the initial lotion bars for Christmas gifts we added bath bombs to our line. We also enjoyed testing them each night!

To enjoy *your* bath even more than before, you too can create these handmade treats with my simple instructions! Bath bombs, tub tabs or **fizzies** (what I prefer to call them) are the effervescent, relaxing treat that fizzes away in your bath like an Alka-Seltzer™ tablet.

Bath bombs are a relatively easy project that anyone can create, novice or master crafter. If you have failed with these in the past, give my recipes a chance and see if you begin to love fizzy making as much as I do. Whether you are making these for yourself, family, friends, or customers, these simple bath treats will take you to **your happy place** after a long day.

Years ago making fizzies took a lot of **trial and error** on my part and I would like to save you that time and frustration by providing this book for anyone with a passion to learn a new skill and have a little fun while doing it. I will warn you in advance, it may be a little frustrating at first, but don't give up; everything takes a little practice and with small adjustments here and there you will be making bath bombs in no time! Forewarning, the spritz and mix step you may have read in tutorials in the past proves to be of great difficulty for many who have tried. I will teach you how to not only avoid this step, but also a lot of trial and error, frustration, and possibly even some tears. Now, let's get to work!

Ingredients

There are two main ingredients you need to make a bath bomb into something that is *fizzy*. One is baking soda, and the other is citric acid. Without these ingredients you will not have any fizz in your fizzy, and that's the fun part! Once you begin to experiment you will find your own unique blend of ingredients to make **your own individual recipe**.

Butters

Butters are a creamy addition to a bath fizzy. With the right combination you can have a moisturizing treat that is so much more than your average store-bought bath bomb. Adding butters will further moisturize your skin, lessening the need for additional lotions. There are many kinds of butter available, ranging from inexpensive to very expensive, such as kokum butter.

Avocado butter: A soft, heavy butter made from crushed avocado fruit. I like to mix avocado butter with cocoa or mango butter when making bath bombs. Caution! Leaves a greasy residue. Use caution as it can make the tub extra slippery.

Cocoa butter: The addition of cocoa butter will make a solid bath bomb. It melts at body temperature right into the skin. Cocoa butter is known to be great for **scars and stretch marks,** and has a lot of **stress relieving** properties. It's very versatile and is also a fantastic choice when making bath melts.

Coffee butter: This butter smells like a fresh brewed cup o' Joe. This will give your bath a little **caffeine boost**. Usually made with coffee seed oil and vegetable oil.

Illipe butter: A little more expensive, but worth the additional cost. It is a very **moisturizing** butter with one downfall, which is that the melting point is higher; therefore you will not want to use a lot of it in your bath bomb recipes.

Kokum butter: A white and flaky butter that is high in fatty acids to **help regenerate new skin cells**. A little goes a long way!

Mango butter: A creamy butter that **prolongs the fizzing** in your typical bath bomb and is also great for bath melts.

Shea butter: Does not leave a greasy residue, but is well absorbed into the skin. When making bath bombs with shea butter, I have noticed after approximately 6 months the scent of the shea butter will come back, but the fragrance oil will dissolve.

Tucuma butter: Pressing the fruit seeds of the tucuma palm tree creates Tucuma butter. It is known for its ability to **combat free radicals** with just enough fatty acids to **moisturize** the skin.

Dry Ingredients

Arrowroot powder: Odorless powder that can be used instead of cornstarch.

Bentonite clay: Very absorbent clay. Use sparingly. **Note:** If you use too much of this ingredient your bath bombs will swell and crack.

Borax: Powdered borax is white, consisting of soft colorless crystals that dissolve easily in water. This is a **water softener** and can be found in the laundry section of many stores.

Citric acid: Citric acid is a common food additive and is found in everything from sodas to candies. It is the ingredient that will **make your bath bomb fizz.** Citric acid and baking soda are both necessary to create a bath fizzy.

Coconut flour: High in lauric acid and has a faint coconut smell.

Cornstarch: The starch derived from the corn (maize) grain, obtained from the endosperm of the corn kernel.

Epsom salts: Epsom salts can play a role in **removing toxins from the body**. Studies have shown that magnesium and sulfates are both readily absorbed through the skin, making Epsom salt baths an easy and ideal way to enjoy the amazing health benefit.

Goat milk powder: Makes a rich and creamy bath fizzy that is very **emollient and nourishing** to the skin. This is a great choice for making winter bath bombs!

Menthol crystals: Cooling and refreshing with a strong minty scent. Adding this ingredient will be excellent in chest rubs, shower steamers, cooling lotions or balms. Keep away from "sensitive" areas and eyes.

Oatmeal: Some recipes in this book will use ground (until a fine powder) oatmeal, also known as colloidal oats. Oatmeal is one of the best ingredients for **itchy and dry skin**.

Rose clay: Mild kaolin clay that can be used on **normal to dry** skin to gently **cleanse and exfoliate** while improving the skin's **circulation**. Rose clay gives a beautiful pink color to soaps and powders.

Sea salt: Helps treat some skin conditions, such as **psoriasis**. Sea salts are also known to relieve **arthritis pain**. Whether you get coarse or fine ground salts is up to you, either will work.

Sodium bicarbonate: This salt has many related names, but almost everyone calls it **baking soda**. A white solid that appears like a fine powder.

Note: This ingredient mixed with citric acid creates the fizzing reaction. Every bath bomb needs this ingredient mixture.

Sodium hydroxide (lye): Also known as caustic soda, but most commonly known as **lye**. It is a necessary ingredient to make true soap.

Sodium lauryl sulfoacetate (SLSA): White powder that is a great alternative to Sodium Lauryl Sulfate, which is a harsh chemical. SLSA is derived from the coconut and palm oils that make the **long lasting bubbles** and **create lather** in bath and body products.

Titanium dioxide: Used in soap making to **whiten** soaps, cosmetics (such as lipstick), the exterior of candles and other toiletries.

Note: Remember to store your properly labeled, sealed ingredients in a cool, dry location away from people, pets, and children.

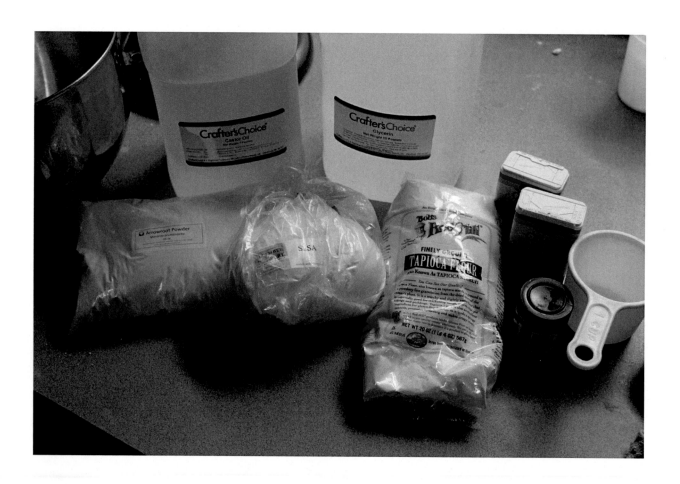

Carrier Oils

Carrier oils are used to dilute essential and fragrance oils. Most are liquid oils with the exception of coconut oil and palm oil, which are solid at room temperature. Keep oils in a cool area at all times to promote a longer shelf life.

Some of the oils are light and feel weightless on the skin, while others are heavy and thick. When adding heavier oils to your recipes make sure to add them in combination with lighter oils to balance the bath bomb ingredients, and prevent puffiness.

Caution!

It is **EXTREMELY IMPORTANT** that you label your product when using **NUT OILS** due to potential life threatening nut allergies.

Apricot oil: Cold-pressed from the dried apricot seeds, light in color, with a nutty scent.

Argan oil: The Argan tree, only found in Morocco, is where this oil begins. It is known to be great for the **skin and hair**.

Avocado oil: Loaded with **proteins, lecithin, beta-carotene and vitamins A, D and E**. The oil is light green/yellow in color.

Castor oil: A vegetable oil that is created by pressing the seeds of the castor plant.

Cherry seed oil: Derived from sour cherry pits left over from juice production. This oil is a great choice for creating products for **acne-prone or inflamed skin** because the oil is said to promote collagen synthesis and **skin healing processes**. Light yellow in color.

Fractionated coconut oil: It is light, odorless and colorless. It absorbs into skin easily and is a natural safe moisturizer that **leaves skin smooth** and not greasy. It can be used with more expensive carrier oils to increase the shelf life of your products.

Grape seed oil: This oil is lightweight, **hypoallergenic** and not greasy.

Hemp seed oil: Aroma of fresh cut grass, best mixed with a heavier oil if applying to skin.

Jojoba oil: Jojoba is akin to liquid gold. Normally found in many high-end products because of its stability, it **nourishes dry and itchy skin**. It is a medium-weight oil.

Olive oil: Not only is this versatile in your kitchen, it is a universal oil in this process as well and is used in a wide range of products. Green/yellow in color.
Note: It has a tendency to go rancid, so it is best used for products that will be used within several months.

Rice bran oil: This oil is a good choice to replace palm oil in recipes. It creates a hard, yet **conditioning, mild** soap and produces a luxurious, creamy lather.

Sweet almond oil: This is a nut oil and you must label your product accordingly. Sweet almond oil is a very soothing golden oil that is made from pressed almonds. It is medium weight and should be used with another oil.

Colors

There are many bath bomb approved colors and you have the choice of using wet or dry coloring for your bath bombs. There are powdered colors, such as **Lake Colors** or **Mica** that can be added to the dry mix. If it is a liquid dye, it should be added to the wet ingredients. Liquid dyes are very concentrated; you only need 1-3 drops per recipe provided. This will keep you from getting specks in your bath bomb.

Use the liquid coloring *sparingly* as it can cause **swelling** in your products because it contains glycerin, which attracts water and even more swelling can occur if you are located in high humidity.

The fizzies shown below are shrink-wrapped, which is also helpful when selling in high humidity (so that your bath bombs are protected from the moisture in the air); especially important if you are selling outdoors!

Here are several color ideas using Lake and Mica coloring.

The Easter Egg Fizzies shown here were molded in plastic Easter eggs.

1/2 cup

Molds

One of my favorite aspects of making bath bombs is that you can be so **creative** with your recipes and imagination! With the use of candy molds, silicone baking molds, cupcake liners, stainless steel molds, and all the little additions (candies, herbs, etc.), you can make just about **anything you dream up**. Here are some ideas to get **your imagination** going.

Note: When using molds for bath bombs, you <u>do not</u> need to oil, grease, or to otherwise treat your molds. The ingredients used to make bath bombs normally do not stick when using a clean, dry mold.

Cake pans: Small pans, such as mini Bundt cake pans are great for those extra special (large) bath bombs.

Candy molds: Head down the cake and candy aisle and see what you can find. These molds are great for **butter melts and embeds** (small items embedded into a bath bomb). Use moderate force to push the mixture firmly into any fine details and to fill in all the edges. Note: Candy molds are not very pliable (usually thin plastic) and make it difficult for mass production.

Christmas ornament packaging: The packaging for bulb ornaments usually works perfectly for bath bombs!

Easter eggs (plastic): These are great for Easter baskets for adults who want something more relaxing than candy-coated eggs. Completed product shown on page 6.

Metal molds: Stainless steel is ideal to work with in the form of a meat baller (as in meat ball sandwich). Stainless steel cups or 2-piece metal bath bomb molds are also great choices.

Paper molds: Cupcake liners, nut cups, and mini bread molds.

Plastic 2-piece molds: The hot new thing that everyone wants to work with! Take your mix, put it in the mold, twist and press to compact, and then it's done! They are a very affordable choice, especially for the new bath bomb maker. A fun treat that you can create with these molds are the Candy Apple Fizzies shown on page 35. They also make a **durable and inexpensive packaging** option.

Plastic 2-part mold 2.75" by Wholesale Supplies Plus.

Silicone molds: Working with silicone is a dream (and great for beginners) because they come in **fun shapes and are easy to unmold**. They are often found in baking and candy aisles, or seasonal areas in the form of ice cube molds.

Snowball maker: Another easy great mold to use, especially for **beginners**.

Snowball maker, mini meat baller, average meat baller.

Essential Oils and Fragrance Oils

Essential oils are naturally scented, and often used for aromatherapy. Fragrance oils are generally inexpensive, are synthetic, but they also expand your scent possibilities more than if you were to only choose to use essential oils. Carefully consider your manufacturer's usage guidelines when adding scents to your recipes.

Use spicy, minty, and menthol oils sparingly!

Wet Ingredients

- Distilled water
- Everclear, vodka or Isopropyl alcohol that is 75 percent or greater
- Witch hazel

Standard Supplies

- Bowls (small, medium, large, extra-large)
- Digital measuring scale (such as a food scale)
- Drying trays lined with paper. The bread racks from restaurant supply stores work great.
- Egg crate (used as bedding cushion) cut and placed on hard surface or trays
- Gloves
- Mask
- Microwave (or double boiler)
- Microwave-safe bowl, cups
- Rubber spatula
- Stand or hand mixer
- Towel(s)
- Wooden skewer/dowel (to scrape bowl while blending)

Workspace

If you are producing other than for yourself, you **MUST wear a hair net and gloves.**

Ensure your workspace is clean and organized.

It is easiest to **measure all ingredients before beginning.**

Recipes

The following recipes will begin with my **Basic Bath Bomb** recipe. From there I will show you my technique for getting the best results while making bath bombs.

The later recipes in this book will be modifications of this recipe, with a bit more flair than the basic bath bomb. You will be making bath bombs with liquor for a little "over 21" fun, herbal, creative molds, cupcakes, pops, truffles, and even candy apples!

Holly's Basic Bath Bomb Recipe

I wanted this to be my first recipe in this book because it's a great recipe for beginners and allows you to use several different butters in one recipe. Fun to make, and fabulous to use!

Mix together:
3 cups baking soda
1 ½ cups citric acid
1 ½ cups cornstarch
3 tablespoons borax

Melt together:
1 ounce mango butter
1 ounce cocoa butter
1.6 ounces grape seed oil

Combine:
½ ounce distilled water
½ ounce clear alcohol
2 tablespoons scent of choice
Bath bomb approved colors

Makes approximately 20-25 average sized bath fizzies.

The following pages will describe my basic bath fizzy recipe in detail with pictures. Use these instructions and my fail-proof tips and tricks to complete the other recipes in this book after you master the basic fizzy.

Tips for All Recipes

- Always break up powdery chucks.
- When using your microwave, make sure your bowl is microwave safe.
- You can generally melt butters and oils with your preference of a double boiler or a microwave.
- Always heat in your microwave slowly, usually 15-30 second spurts of heating at a time, depending on your wattage.
- Test by squeezing mixture to ensure it can hold shape and feels like wet sand.
- Mold and let harden overnight, unless otherwise stated.

1. Mix all **powders** together in a stand mixer, placing a towel over the machine to prevent powders from escaping while stirring; set aside.

2. Mix **butters** and **oil** and melt in a double boiler or microwave until completely melted; set aside.

3. Next, mix **water**, **alcohol**, **scent** and **color** in a small bowl.

4. Combine the **water** mixture with the **oil** mixture once the butters and oil have **cooled to touch** but are not completely cold, leaving the mixture **slightly warm**. If it cools too much the butters will solidify and make it difficult to blend.

5. With mixer on **low**, pour liquids **into dry mixture** with **a steady stream**. If you move slowly the mixture has an opportunity to react and start to fizz.

6. **Increase speed slightly**, by one notch, to mix well. Again, this is to incorporate the mixture as quickly as possible to **prevent the fizzing reaction** that combining the ingredients can create. Once mixed well, turn mixer speed back to **low to prevent drying**, mixing for an additional 1-2 minutes.

7. Use **skewer** to scrape the inside of the bowl to fully incorporate butters into mixture.

8. **Test** by squeezing the mixture to ensure it can **hold its shape** and feels like **wet sand**.

9. **Fill** chosen mold with mixture.

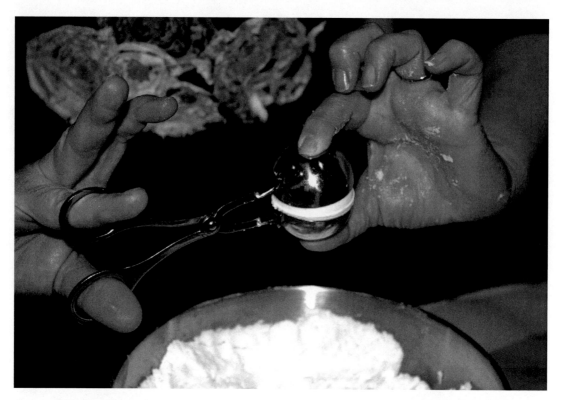

10. **Squeeze mold** with fingers so that your fingers are pressing the mixture firmly.

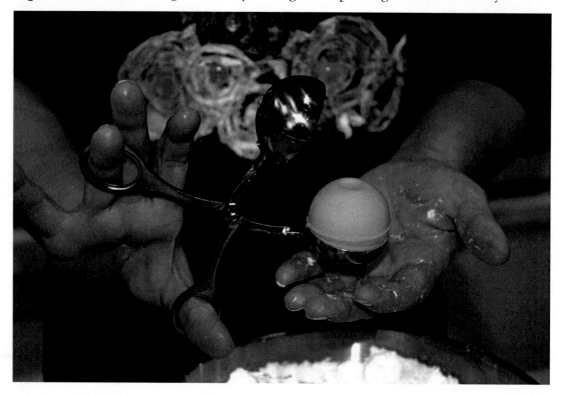

Shown above made with a **snowball maker** and below removed from a **steel mold.**

Happy Hour Fizzy

෧෨෧෨෧෨෧෨෧෨෧෨෧෨෧෨

Don't be tempted to drink the tub water after sitting in this indulgent bath. Although, who could blame you if you had a little taste of some tequila while making these? They are a great favor/gift for bachelorette parties, bridesmaid gifts, girls' weekends, housewarming, or just about any party! It's 5 'o clock somewhere!

Mix together:
3 cups baking soda
1 ½ cups citric acid
1 ½ cups arrowroot powder
2 tablespoons dried lemon
and lime zest

Melt together:
2 ounces lime butter
1.6 ounces grape seed oil

Combine:
½ ounce distilled water
½ ounce 100-proof tequila
¾ ounce lime essential oil

Makes approximately 20-25 average sized bath fizzies.

Mix powders together, and combine with mixer on low. Add dried lemon and lime zest. Continue mixing until well blended. Mix butter and oil, and melt in a double boiler or microwave until completely melted; set aside.

Next, mix water, tequila and essential oil in a small bowl. Once butters have cooled slightly, combine the water and oil mixtures together.

With mixer on low, pour liquids **into dry mixture** and increase speed slightly (by one notch); mix well. Turn mixer to low, mixing for an additional 1-2 minutes.

Salt, please:
Melt a small amount of white melt and pour soap and let cool until it *just starts to thicken*. Take a bath bomb, dip one side in the melted soap, and then dip the same side into a small amount of coarse salt. *Bottoms up*!

Testimonial:

I loathe everything about making bath bombs.... Strike that, I used to loathe it. When I met Holly, she introduced me to her magical way of preparing the perfect bath bomb. Each recipe I've tried has been outstanding, so easy to work with. No more cracks, warting or wonky bath bombs. The 'Swear Jar' is getting a break in my household now thanks to Holly's genius!"

Tanya Rasley
Baby Duck Soap Co.
www.babyducksoap.com

Lemoncello Fizzy

❧❧❧❧❧❧❧❧❧❧

A refreshing lemon bath bomb, for a relaxing summer evening.

Mix together:
3 cups baking soda
1 ½ cups citric acid
1 ½ cups cornstarch
Yellow bath bomb color

Melt together:
1 ounce lemon butter
1 ounce Illipe butter
1.6 ounces apricot kernel oil

Combine:
½ ounce distilled water
½ ounce vodka
¾ ounce lemon essential oil

Makes approximately 20-25 average sized bath fizzies.

Mix dry ingredients together in a stand mixer and mix on low (placing a towel over the machine to prevent powders from escaping). Mix butters and oil and melt in a double boiler or in the microwave until completely melted; set aside. Next, mix water, alcohol and essential oil in a small bowl. Once butters and oil have cooled, combine the water mixture and oil mixture.

With mixer on low, pour liquids into dry mixture and increase speed slightly (one notch); mix well. Turn mixer to low, mixing for an additional 1-2 minutes.

Oatmeal & Milk Winter Fizzy

If winter has your skin itchy and dry then this will be the perfect choice for an addition to your nice, warm bath! Indulge in these to sooth your winter skin.

Mix together:
5 cups baking soda
1 cup powdered goat's milk
3 cups citric acid
2 cups cornstarch
1 cup ground (colloidal) oats

Melt together:
2 ounces shea butter
2 ounces mango butter
3.2 ounces avocado oil

Combine:
1 ounce distilled water
1 ounce clear alcohol
4 tablespoons honey
scent

Makes approximately 45-50 average sized bath fizzies.

Mix all powders together in a stand mixer (placing a towel over the machine to prevent powders from escaping). Mix butters and oil; melt in a double boiler or in the microwave until completely melted; set aside. Next mix water, alcohol and scent in a small bowl. When butters and oil have cooled combine the water mixture and oil mixture together.

With mixer on low, pour liquids into dry mixture and increase speed slightly (one notch), making sure to mix well. Turn mixer down to low, mixing for an additional 1-2 minutes.

To make **colloidal oats**, take 2 cups of old-fashioned or instant oats and grind in food processor until a fine powder.

Herbal Bath Fizzy

An herbal bath fizzy is quite the treat. Not only do you get a bath fizzy, you also get a bath tea with flower petals, such as dried roses or lavender buds in your water.

Mix together:
3 cups baking soda
1 ½ cups citric acid
1 cup arrowroot powder
½ cup rose clay

Melt together:
2 ounces kokum butter
1.6 ounces jojoba oil

Combine:
½ ounce water
½ ounce alcohol
¾ ounce lavender & rose essential oils (combined weight to obtain desired scent)

Into mold:
Dried roses, pinch   or   Dried lavender buds, pinch

Tip! A _little_ goes a **long** way!

Makes approximately 20-25 average sized bath fizzies.

Mix all powders together in a stand mixer (placing a towel over the machine to prevent powders from escaping). Melt butter and oil together in a double boiler or in the microwave until completely melted; set aside. Next, mix water, alcohol and scent in a small bowl. Mix lavender and rose oils to your preference. Once butter and oil have cooled; combine the water mixture and oil mixture together.

With mixer on low, pour liquids into dry mixture and increase speed slightly (by one notch), making sure to mix well. Turn mixer to low, mixing for an additional 1-2 minutes.

Dried flower and herb addition:
Before pressing mixture into a mold or machine, place a pinch of dried herbs and/or roses in the bottom of the mold to accent your bath bomb. When it dissolves they will float in the water.

No-Butter Bombs

⋖⋗⋖⋗⋖⋗⋖⋗⋖⋗⋖⋗⋖⋗⋖⋗

No butter, no problem; you can make these bath bombs without it. Adding cherry kernel oil will offer similar conditioning results with moisturizing oils.

Mix together:
2 ½ cups baking soda
1 cup tapioca starch
1 ½ cups citric acid
½ teaspoon borax

Melt together:
2 teaspoons witch hazel
2 tablespoons cherry kernel oil
1 teaspoon each of lavender and chamomile essential oils
1 teaspoon liquid blue colorant (optional)

Makes approximately 12-15 average sized bath fizzies.

Mix powders together in a stand mixer (placing a towel over the machine to prevent powders from escaping). Mix the witch hazel, cherry kernel oil, scent and color into a cup, mix well to combine.

Pour **half** of liquid into the bowl with the dry mix, quickly stir by hand to blend it in. Add **other half** of liquid into mix and blend until the mixture is all one color and has the texture of **wet sand**. Once mixed in, it will **hold together when squeezed**.

Note: The rest of the process includes the use of a bath bomb machine, if you have one. If you do not, proceed with desired mold. Ensure you are following the proper usage instructions and guidelines included in the instruction manual of your machine.

Once the bath bombs are complete, according to machine directions, place onto a drying rack until hard.

Tropical Escape Fizzy

⤜⤐⤜⤐⤜⤐⤜⤐⤜⤐⤜⤐⤜⤐⤜⤐

This relaxing bath bomb will send your mind day dreaming on a tropical island with an umbrella-accented, fruity cocktail in hand. The Tropical Escape uses mango butter and avocado oil for a smooth, luxurious feel. Mango butter is semi-soft and non-greasy which makes it a great moisturizer while the avocado oil is high in vitamin E, which is widely suggested to protect and repair the skin.

Mix together:
6 cups baking soda
3 cups citric acid
2 cups cornstarch
1 cup kaolin clay
3 tablespoons borax

Mix together:
4 ounces mango butter
3.2 ounces avocado oil
1 ounce clear alcohol
1 ounce distilled water
4 tablespoons Hawaiian ginger scent

Makes approximately 40-50 average sized bath fizzies.

Using a stand mixer (placing a towel over the machine to prevent powders from escaping), add the dry ingredients to the bowl and cover with a towel. Turn mixer on low and let mix for about 3-5 minutes. In a microwave safe bowl, add the mango butter and avocado oil and heat in spurts until melted; set aside.

Combine alcohol, water and scent. Once oils have cooled, add the alcohol mixture to the oil mixture and stir to combine. With the mixer on low, pour all the wet ingredients in and turn up a couple notches to incorporate all ingredients quickly. Once combined, mix on low for approximately 1 additional minute. Turn mixer off.

Use your desired mold to finish the bath bombs.

Testimonial:
Love these bath bombs, so easy to do once you have a great recipe. Holly gives clear, step-by-step instructions for the best no-fail bath bombs ever!

Angela Carillo
www.alegnasoap.com

Surprise Inside (bath melts or toy)

The following two recipes include a surprise inside. You can use a bath melt or a small plastic toy. If using a bath melt as a surprise, you must make them <u>before</u> your bath bomb mix.

Use your favorite fizzy recipe, or the following one, to create the bath bombs. After these bath bombs have fizzed away in your bath the user will find a surprise in the middle.

Surprise Melts

Melt 1 cup of cocoa butter (or more, depending on how many you would like to make) in a microwave. Add mica for color (optional). Mix together until combined well. Pour mixture into small (smaller than your bath bomb) fun silicone molds. Let cool and pop out of mold. Set aside. Next, make bath bomb recipe of choice.

Makes approximately 45-50 average sized bath fizzies.

Mix together:
6 cups baking soda
3 cups citric acid
3 cups cornstarch
4 tablespoons borax

Melt together:
3.2 ounces avocado oil
2 ounces shea butter
2 ounces mango butter

Combine:
1 ounce distilled water
1 ounce clear alcohol
4 tablespoons fruity scent
1 teaspoon mica coloring (optional)

Mix all powders together in a stand mixer. Mix butters with oil; heat in a double boiler or in the microwave until completely melted; set aside. Next, mix water, alcohol and scent in a small bowl. When butters and oil have cooled; combine the water mixture and oil mixture together.

Fill **half** of your bath bomb mold with the mixture and place your melt in middle. Continue filling the mold with more of the mixture until completely full. Squeeze tight! Remove from mold and place on a lined rack to dry.

For Kids: Add a small toy or little fish inside in place of melt, keeping it smaller than a quarter.

Caution! Make sure to label any small items inserted into this recipe with **'choking hazard'**!
Caution! The oil in this recipe can create **slickness** in the bathtub.

Toys

Fill **half** of your mold with the mixture and place your toy in middle. Continue filling the mold with more of the mixture until completely full. Squeeze tight! Remove from mold and place on a lined rack to dry.

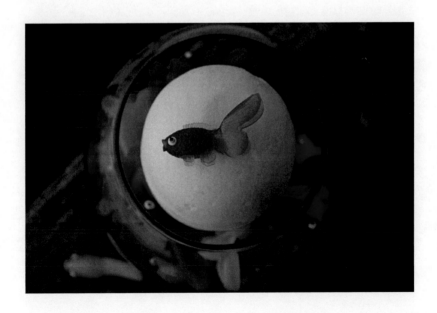

Pops, Truffles & Candy Apples

You may have to make a warning label with these *delicious* looking bath treats! Even though you'll **want to eat them up**, please *refrain*! These goodies are fun for all ages, and a thoughtful gift for the sweet lovers in your life!

Ingredients & Supplies

Completed truffle sized bath bombs from your favorite recipe.

Sprinkles	Lollipop sticks	Popsicle sticks
Mini paper cups	Lollipop bags	Microwave safe dish
White melt and pour soap (¼ - ½ cup per recipe)		Packaging of choice

Fizzy Pops

Make a batch of bath bombs according to previous directions from your favorite recipe (smaller round molds, such as a mini meat baller will make these look more realistic). Slowly place a lollipop stick into the middle of each 'pop'. Once **dry,** you may continue to the dipping phase of the project.

Dipping

Cut the melt and pour soap into small chunks and melt slowly in the microwave, just as if you were making the chocolate for edible truffles. While that is melting in the microwave, poke each bath fizzy with a lollipop stick. Remove the melt and pour soap from the microwave to begin dipping.

Temporarily remove the lollipop stick, dip stick into the melted soap and place back into the fizzy. The soap will act as an adhesive for the stick to stay in the bath fizzy while dipping. Dip fizzy into the liquid melt and pour soap and continue to the decorating step below.

Decorating

While the melt and pour soap is still warm, dip the fizzy into sprinkles, dots, candies, jojoba beads or whatever other creative add-ons that you can think of. Let the 'pop' dry upright in Styrofoam or an empty box with holes for the sticks works well also. Once they have dried you can complete the look by placing a clear lollipop bag over each one and tying with a cute ribbon.

Truffles

❧❧❧❧❧

Truffles are thought of as a special treat for most people. These truffles are no different! They can be created into the most adorable box of bath treats that you can imagine. How could your friends not be in love with their new gift? Make sure to label them so no one tries to eat 'em up!

Complete the previous directions for **Fizzy Pops** (with the exception of the lollipop stick steps). Place your bath truffle in small/mini paper cups (truffle cups).

Candy Apple Fizzies

Candy Apples shown here can be made by using a larger (2.75") mold, replacing lollipop sticks with popsicle sticks (or candy apple sticks) and by using red, brown or caramel coloring to tint the melt and pour soap to look like a candy apple or a chocolate and caramel apple.

Cupcake Fizzies

❧❧❧❧❧❧❧❧❧❧

By the time you reach this recipe you should be a pro and are already looking for more challenging and fun bath bombs to make. Look no further, and try this cupcake recipe to show off all your new skills! Don't let this one intimidate you by the amount of steps; it's a really fun bath bomb to make!
No one can resist a cupcake!

These are a great gift for the cupcake lover in your life, or even to sell to cupcake shops and bakeries.

Mix together:	**Mix together:**	**Combine:**
3 cups baking soda	1 ounce shea butter	½ ounce distilled water
1 ½ cups citric acid	1 ounce cocoa butter	½ ounce alcohol
1 ½ cups cornstarch	1.6 ounces grape seed oil	2 tablespoons desired scent

Note: Pick a fragrance that does <u>not</u> contain <u>vanilla</u>, as it will discolor in time.

1 teaspoon of bath bomb color

Makes approximately 8-10 average cupcake sized bath fizzies.

Additional Supplies

- Cake decorating tip(s)
- Glitter (because a little glitter never hurt anyone)
- Icing/piping bags (or a thicker sandwich bag with small cut in corner for the tip)
- Scissors
- Several additional containers for mixing and ingredients (depending on recipe)
- Silicone cupcake molds, nut cups or cupcake liners in a cupcake tin
- Sprinkles, sprinkles, and more sprinkles!
- Titanium dioxide (if you are making the Cold Process Soap Topping)

Make your desired bath bombs according to directions from your favorite recipe. Press mix *firmly* into the cupcake molds of your choice and set aside to dry while you make your topping.

There are several options for the cupcake topping; Cold-Process Soap Topping, Royal Icing Sugar Scrub Topping, or the Whipped Soap Topping. The choice is yours and you will find some of my favorite recipes listed here.

Cold Process Soap Topping

❧☙❧☙❧☙❧☙❧☙❧☙❧☙❧☙❧☙❧☙❧☙

When you add this topping to a cupcake fizzy the user gets a small bar of soap to use after the bath fizzy has dissolved! Use your favorite recipe for the soap topping, or the one below.
This recipe is intended to be made by **adults only!**
Contains **caustic** materials (lye).

Special Supplies

In addition to the standard supplies listed in the beginning of this book, you will also need the following supplies to work with lye:

- Heavy duty, heat-safe <u>plastic</u> container, not glass
- Immersion blender (also known as a stick/wand blender)
- Labeled spray bottle with pure vinegar
- Lye pitcher (such as a heavy duty plastic drink pitcher)
- Spatula

<u>NEVER USE CONTAINERS FOR FOOD PREPARATION AFTER THEY HAVE BEEN USED FOR LYE</u>

If you have already made soap in the past, you may use one of your own recipes or the one provided for you here. This recipe uses **lye** and you **MUST** wear goggles and gloves! * See <u>Lye Safety</u> (next page) if you are not familiar with working with lye.

Mix together:
9.3 ounces distilled water
4.6 ounces lye

Melt together:
2 ounces shea butter
12 ounces coconut oil

Mix together:
14 ounces olive oil
4 ounces rice bran oil

Combine:
Shea butter/coconut oil mixture
Olive oil/Rice bran oil mixture
2 tablespoons titanium dioxide

1 ½ ounces scent (Note: Vanilla will discolor over time)

With goggles and gloves on, add the distilled water in a heat safe plastic **(NOT GLASS)** container.

Caution! Keep lye in a container marked "POISON" where children and animals cannot access it. Always remember to work in a well-ventilated area when working with lye!

In a separate cup, measure the lye. Slowly **pour lye into the water** and stir using a rubber spatula; mixing the lye and water well. If you are using water-soluble titanium dioxide, add to the lye pitcher and stir well.

Always add lye to the water; never add water to the lye!

While lye is cooling, melt coconut oil and shea butter in the microwave. Set aside to cool. Next, place olive oil and rice bran oil into a **stainless steel** pot. Combine with shea butter and coconut oil mixture. Stir to combine. If you are using oil-soluble titanium dioxide, add to melted oils. Add scent to the oils; stirring to blend completely.

Take your cooled lye solution and **slowly pour into oils**; stirring by hand to mix well (approximately 1 minute).

Next, take the immersion blender and blend mixture with short bursts of power until fully combined. A spatula can assist with this to clean the sides of the bowl, alternating between them to blend well. Ensure that you have blended the oils so there isn't any separation or floating oil in the mixture. The mixture should have a thick pudding consistency, also known as **TRACE**.

Note: When making bar soap you would stop here, but we are taking it a step further so the soap will sit on top of the cupcake and not run down the sides.

Continue with the immersion blender in short spurts of power every 30-seconds until hard peaks form (similar to meringue pie topping) when you pull the blender out of the mixture the soap mixture will keep its shape.

Lye Safety

If you get **lye on flesh**, immediately wash with soap and water. After you wash completely, spray vinegar on the area (not in eyes). **NEVER** spray vinegar on lye, **always wash first!**

The exothermic reaction caused by mixing vinegar and lye will burn hot and fast.

If you get **lye in the eyes**, flush with water for several minutes and seek medical attention immediately.

If you spill a lye solution **on a surface** or want to neutralize equipment/utensils used with lye, use the spray bottle of vinegar (acts as a neutralizer).

Remember, once you have used something with lye, it should **never** be used for food again.

To decorate the cupcakes

Cut tip off icing/piping bag and insert decorating tip, pushing it all the way down to fit tightly in the corner. Fill with the 'icing' (cold process soap) mixture.

Begin in the center by squeezing mixture in the middle to build a foundation for the remaining 'icing'. Top the cupcake as you would an edible cupcake, by adding sprinkles or other decorations to the top.

Let cure for **4-6 weeks**. After curing it is safe to use.
Important: You are working with raw soap. It can **<u>burn you</u>** if it comes in contact with skin.

Royal Icing Sugar Scrub Topping pictured below.

Royal Icing Sugar Scrub Topping

When the topping floats off the 'cupcake' it's a ready-made body scrub! It is two bath treats in one!

The fizzy dissolves.

Note: These should dry for 24-48 hours before using or wrapping.

Stir together:
1 ¾ cups powdered sugar
4 ½ teaspoons meringue powder
¼ teaspoon cream of tartar
Add a teaspoon of color (optional)

Mix together:
¼ cup warm water
½ teaspoon essential oil
1 teaspoon color (optional)

Hand stir into mixture:
½ cup granulated sugar

Tops approximately 6-8 average sized cupcakes.

In a stand mixer, stir together powder ingredients. Mix warm water and scent, add to dry mixture. Beat with electric mixer on low until combined. Hand stir in granulated sugar.

Beat on high for approximately 7-10 minutes, or until **very stiff**.

Cut tip off icing/piping bag and insert decorating tip, pushing all the way down to fit tightly in the corner. Fill with the 'icing' mixture.

Top the cupcake as you would an edible cupcake, by adding sprinkles or other decorations to the top.

The topping makes a scrub.

Whipped Soap Topping

You may have to make a few batches of this topping, depending on how much you put on each cupcake. This topping hardens faster than the others, so remember to **work quickly**.

Melt:
8 ounces melt and pour soap base

Stir in:
8 ounces foaming bath whip

Add in:
½ ounce scent (Note: If you use <u>vanilla</u> it will discolor)
1 ounce castor oil
½ teaspoon color (optional)

Cut the melt and pour soap into small squares and place in a microwave safe bowl. Heat in microwave in short spurts taking into consideration the wattage of your microwave. DO NOT OVERHEAT! Stir in foaming bath whip, until *mostly* melted.

With mixer, mix on low until it starts getting **thicker**, but *not too thick*. Add scent, color (optional), and castor oil. Blend until whipped.

Fill piping bag and top cupcakes with the whipped topping; work quickly. Let stand for 24 hours to completely harden.

Note: Soaps shown below (and opposite page) are made with the Whipped Soap Topping on top of a dyed melt and pour base, inside a small plastic cup with a monster bath toy on top. This little monster can stay in the tub!

Bubble Gum Bubbly Bars

❧❧❧❧❧❧❧❧❧❧❧❧❧❧

Bubble Bars are **so much fun** and add color and **lots and lots of bubbles** to your bath, unlike bath bombs, which do not bubble (unless you add SLSA - Sodium Lauryl Sulfoacetate).

Mix together:
2 cups baking soda
1 ½ cups cornstarch
2 cups SLSA
1 1/3 cups cream of tartar
Body safe liquid colorant

Mix together:
1 ½ cups glycerin
2 tablespoons fractionated coconut oil

Mix together:
2 tablespoons tapioca starch
1 ½ tablespoons bubble gum (or other) fragrance oil

Makes approximately 8 1-ounce bars.

This recipe contains SLSA (Sodium Lauryl Sulfoacetate), therefore <u>you MUST wear a mask until completely mixed.</u> Caution! Make sure to label all of your products made with SLSA as it can be irritating, especially to those with sensitive skin.

Miscellaneous Supplies

- Additional containers to separate mixture.

Mix powder ingredients in a stand mixer (placing a towel over the machine to prevent powders from escaping), stirring well and set aside. In a small cup mix the tapioca starch and your scent together, after blended add to your dry ingredients. Hand mix **with gloved hands** until incorporated. Next, add glycerin and coconut oil to combined mixture, stirring it well **by hand** (mix and squish motion similar to making bread dough) until it's combined into a small ball.

Coloring

Split your 'dough' into **two containers** and drop desired color into each mixture, mixing again by hand. Blend the color throughout the 'dough' until completely incorporated.

The picture to the right used Bath Bomb Blue Powder Color and Bath Bomb Yellow Powder Color.

Once combined, on a piece of wax paper, flatten 'dough' of one color of the mixture into a rectangle.

This will be the outside color.

Next, take the other color and flatten, pictured below. Place on top of bottom layer, pictured to the right, shown here in yellow.

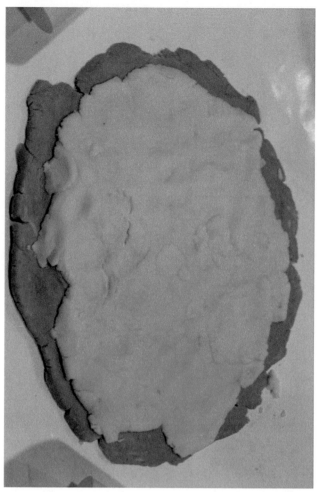

Cutting

Finally, roll it like a log sandwich roll in a tortilla, or a sushi roll. Take one side of the paper and pull up and over, and pull towards yourself real tight. Keeping it tight, roll until it is in the shape of a log, being careful not to roll the paper into the log. Place on a **new** piece of paper and let rest for **2 hours**. It will firm up during this time.

The Bubbly Bars shown on page 44 were scooped with an ice cream scoop instead of cutting.

With a **sharp knife** and make slices approximately every **one inch** and place on a **paper-lined baking sheet** to let dry for **several days,** turning every day or two until they are firm.

These are so much fun; once you make one batch you will want to make several batches in different colors!

Directions for use: Break one (1-ounce) bar in half, and then crumble half of bar under running warm water, moving water back and forth to create the bubbles!

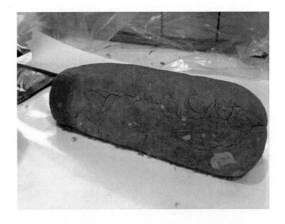

Shown here with blue and magenta red coloring.

Testimonial:
Holly Port is truly the BBQ aka Bath Bomb Queen!

Before her tips and tricks, I was only make a 5 fizzy batch. Now I am making 15-20 bath fizzies at a time. Love that she thinks outside the box by using the different types of ingredients like not using the traditional witch hazel. A stand mixer, and Holly Port's book will be the secret to your bath bomb success.
Michelle Arce
www.madewithlotsoflove.com

Fizzies for Kids

Kids love things that fizz, and bubble. Sprinkling 'Zombie Acid' and 'Fairy Dust' in the tub will add a little additional excitement for bath time fun!

Caution! DO NOT ADD A LOT OF COLOR! The bathtub will need additional cleaning from residual color stains. Unfortunately, a cleaning fairy does not come with the fairy dust.

Zombie Acid

Ingredients:
4 cups mix (from recipe of your choice)
1 teaspoon red bath bomb color

Mix together; bag up in fun zombie themed bags, or standard clear plastic sandwich bags. Label with ingredients. Watch the surprise when the bath water turns red!

(Pictured to the right.)

Directions for use: Add approximately half a cup of mixture to running bath water.

Fairy Dust

Ingredients:
4 cups mix (from recipe of your choice)
1 teaspoon pink bath bomb color
½ teaspoon body-safe glitter

Watch the surprise when the bath water turns pink and glittery!

Directions for use: Add approximately half a cup of mixture to running bath water.

RUN!

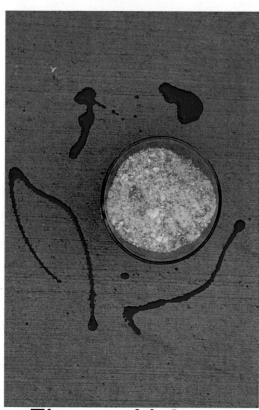

The zombies are

Bubbles, Bubbles, Fizz, Fizz

୬ଈ ୬ଈ ୬ଈ ୬ଈ ୬ଈ ୬ଈ

With this recipe the user gets a little more bubble with their bubbles. To create them all you have to do is vigorously move the water back and forth in the tub.

This recipe contains SLSA (Sodium Lauryl Sulfoacetate), therefore <u>you MUST wear a mask until completely mixed.</u>

Caution! Make sure to label all of your products made with SLSA as it can be irritating, especially to those with sensitive skin.

Makes approximately 20-25 average sized bath fizzies.

Mix together:
3 cups baking soda
1 cup citric acid
1 cup tapioca starch
1 cup (SLSA) Sodium Lauryl Sulfoacetate
1 teaspoon color powder (optional)

Melt together:
1 ounce coconut oil (76 degrees)
1 ounce cocoa butter
1.6 ounces fractionated coconut oil

Combine:
½ ounce water
½ ounce clear alcohol
¼ ounce desired scent

Mix all powder ingredients in a stand mixer (placing a towel over the machine to prevent powders from escaping), and mix on low. In a microwave safe bowl in the microwave, melt oil and butters together, mixing to combine. Let cool for several minutes. In a separate bowl, mix water, alcohol and scent together. Add to butter mixture.

With mixer on low, pour liquids into dry mixture and increase speed slightly (one notch), making sure to mix well. Turn mixer down to low, mixing for an additional 1-2 minutes.

Fun fizzy-making options:

To make your bath fizzies even more **colorful** make another batch of the same mix with another color (or leave it natural) to have a 2-color bath bomb (shown above).

Another option is to place a color on each side of your mold, so when pressed together you have a two color split.

Hippie Lovers

⋘⋘⋘⋘⋘⋘⋘⋘

Peace, love and happiness. This recipe is not your stereotypical patchouli scent that you think of when you hear the word "hippie"! It has a more subdued scent with ylang ylang, sandalwood and orange essential oils.

Mix together:
3 cups baking soda
1 cup citric acid
½ cup Epsom salt
1 ½ cup cornstarch

Melt together:
1.6 ounces hemp oil
1 ounce tucuma butter
1 ounce kokum butter

Combine:
½ ounce distilled water
½ ounce clear alcohol
¼ ounce each of ylang ylang, sandalwood and orange essential oils

Makes approximately 20-25 average sized bath fizzies.

Mix powders and Epsom salt together in a stand mixer (placing a towel over the machine to prevent powders from escaping). Mix butters and oil in a double boiler on medium heat or in the microwave until completely melted; set aside. Next, mix water, alcohol and essential oil in a small bowl. When butters and oils have cooled, combine the water mixture and oil mixture together.

With mixer on low, pour liquid mixture into dry mixture and increase speed slightly (one notch); mix well. Turn mixer to low, mixing for an additional 1-2 minutes.

Chris's Shower Steamers

This is one of my **Amazing Assistant's** recipes. He loves using them in a **warm shower** when he **has a cold**. The menthol, peppermint and eucalyptus aid in opening the sinuses, while the cocoa butter helps keep steamers hard and to last longer in your shower.

Pro tip! I like to press these into unique and different shapes (that I do not use with any other product) so people do not confuse them with bath bombs.

Mix together:
6 cups baking soda
3 cups citric acid
1 cup kaolin clay
2 cups arrowroot powder

Melt together:
4 ounces cocoa butter
3.2 ounces avocado oil

Combine:
1 ounce water
1 ounce alcohol
¾ ounces each of peppermint and eucalyptus essential oils

Add-in:
2 tablespoons menthol crystals

Mix all powders together. Mix butter and oil in a double boiler on medium heat or in the microwave until completely melted; set aside. Next mix water, alcohol, and essential oils in a small bowl. Once butter and oil have cooled, combine the water mixture and oil mixture together.

With mixer on low, pour liquids **into dry mixture** and increase speed slightly (by one notch); mix well. Turn mixer to low, slowly add menthol crystals, mixing for an additional 1-2 minutes to thoroughly blend in the crystals.

Directions for use: In a warm shower, place one shower steamer on floor of shower where warm water will flow directly onto steamer. Relax and let the essential oils and menthol help you get some much-needed fresh (scented) air!

Caution! This recipe contains menthol crystals, which are **not pleasant** on the skin. Be sure to label accordingly.
"Not for the bath, skin, or to come in contact with sensitive areas or eyes"

Milk Baths

The powdered milk added to this bath soak provides a creamy feel,
while the oats help with dry itchy skin.

Fizzing Oatmeal

Ingredients:
4 cups mix (from recipe of your choice)
1 cup colloidal oats
2 cups powdered milk

Herbal Fizzy

Ingredients:
4 cups mix (from recipe of your choice)
4 cups Epson salts
2 -3 tablespoons dried herbs, roses,
chamomile or lavender buds

Mix together, package in clear bags, jars, or containers.

Directions for use: Add approximately half a cup to running bath water and soak for 15-20
minutes.

Potty Bombs

❧❧❧❧❧❧❧❧❧

The potty, toilet, or porcelain god (depending on what you may have done the night before) gets a little stinky from time to time. These Potty Bombs are a great way to **freshen and clean** the bowl with minimal effort. It's always nice to have a batch on hand for the Friday night get-together, last minute guests, or even in a gift basket full of housewarming gifts!

Simply drop one in the toilet and let it rest for **10-15 minutes** while it fizzes away the germs in your toilet bowl. Swish with a brush, or just leave it to go down with the next flush.

The bathroom will smell fresh and clean for hours.

Mix together:
1 cup baking soda
¼ cup citric acid

Mix together:
1 tablespoon hydrogen peroxide
½ teaspoon vinegar
20-30 drops of essential oils

Makes approximately 8-10 small sized potty bombs.

Mix dry ingredients in a medium bowl by hand. Mix the liquid ingredients together into a small separate bowl. *Slowly* add wet mixture into the dry mixture, about a **tablespoon** at a time. Make sure to blend well with **both hands as you go**.

Caution! You must add the liquid slowly or the mixture will create foam.

Working **quickly**, press mixture into small silicone molds and let rest for an hour, or until hard. Pop out from mold and let harden overnight. Place your new loo cleaners in a decorative jar in your newly freshened bathroom.

If you sell them make sure to clearly label them "NOT for bath or body".

In the picture shown I used orange, lavender and tea tree. You can try this blend or choose a refreshing combination that is right for you.

Testimonial:
I'm a mommy of 5 kids, who doesn't have time for long relaxing baths. Until... I used Lotion Bar Cafe's bath fizzies!! Have you tried this thing??? If you haven't you have no idea what you're missing!!! I find time to have my baths with those wonderful fizzies!! Even if it means putting the kids to bed 15 minutes early!!
Jena Bajza

Packaging

I package most of my fizzies in fun and colorful tissue paper with each end twisted to secure the bath bomb like a sweet candy.

Here are some packaging ideas to seal your bath bombs for your friends, family, and customers. Take a look back through the book and review the packaging shown in the pictures.

- Naked – do nothing!
- Shrink-wrap and add a cute label.
- Paper bags with ribbon and a tag.
- Clear cello (cellophane) bags tied with ribbon.
- Wrapped in tissue paper or decorative thin wrapping paper, twisted on the ends.
- Cellophane wrap tied with ribbon – made in a variety of colors, including iridescent.
- Baking boxes, candy boxes (examples, truffle boxes and cupcake boxes)
- Long plastic bags, such as pretzel bags, tied with string.

Frequently Asked Questions

Q: How do I prevent the **powder mess**?

A: My solution to this problem is quite simple – drape a small towel over your mixer, like so:

Q: What do you do with **leftovers**?

A: Save any leftovers to add to the fizzy soak recipe. You can crumble your leftovers and place in small bags (½ cup per soak). If you would like, you can also give some to friends, family and customers as testers for feedback on your new recipe.
Note: Be cognizant of scents, making sure to blend complimenting scents together when using leftovers or wonky batches in new recipes.

Q: What happens if a **batch went wrong**?
A: Yeah, it happens. Something is too wonky to work with, so now what? The good news is that you can make some of the amazing bath soaks with it!

Q: Should I use a **mold maker** or make them **by hand**?

A: I am often asked this, Do *you* want to buy a machine? This is a really personal decision based on your own needs.

At this time, we do ours by hand. One time, my husband and I had a competition where we worked together to see who could make the most fizzies - one by hand and the other by machine. At the end of the race, we were roughly the same pace.

Machine:

- Some require the use of an air compressor (which can be loud).
- The ability to have custom molds made.
- Less wear on your own body.
- Packed tight.
- Price ranges from ~ $275.00 - $900.00.

Hand:

- Cost effective, free!
- You can use a variety of molds, plastic or metal.
- Costs for molds range from approximately 2.00-15.00 per mold.
- No electricity required (I run off espresso).

While you become adjusted to with working with these materials you may run into a few of the common problems the bath bomb pioneers have dealt with before you. The following questions and answers are also to help troubleshoot issues you may have experienced. If you have cracked, warty, growing, or swelling bath bombs that simply will not hold shape, read on!

Q: How do I get my bath bombs to stop **cracking**?

A: When there is too much clay, salt or another dry ingredient, you may have cracking. Measure more carefully for your next batch.

Q: I live in a place with **high humidity** and I've always had problems when trying these in the past. Do you have any tips for me to try again?

A: I sure do!

- After molding, place on a clean tray or hard surface then place a towel over bath bombs.
- Keep away from air conditioning or humidifier and never in the freezer.
- Place in a closet or on drying rack.
- Place on a foam egg crate (similar to mattress toppers). You may want to cut it to fit your allocated space. **Pro tip:** This helps soft bath bombs keep their shape.
- When bath bombs are hard, shrink-wrap to protect them from the moisture in the air.
- Do not overuse salts (Epsom, sea, etc.) in your recipe as salt draws moisture.

Q: What do I do when the mixture **won't stick**?

A: Unfortunately, this can be caused by several factors. Please take into consideration the recipe you used in correlation with the following possibilities and make the appropriate adjustments.

- Too much oil
- Too heavy an oil
- Not enough dry ingredients

Put the batch back in the mixer and blend for a few additional minutes. The blending helps it dry and will allow you to re-mold your mixture.

Q: How do I fix my mixture when it feels **too wet?**

A: Your mixture should feel like wet sand. If it feels too wet simply put back in the mixer and add 1-2 tablespoons of cornstarch or clay at a time. Continue re-mixing until it resembles wet sand.

Q: How do I fix my mixture when my bath bombs start **growing and swelling**?

A: Any growth and swelling is usually due to too much moisture (either in the mix or the environment, if you are located somewhere with high humidity).

Q: Why do my bath bombs have **wart** looking bumps on them?

A: Wart-like bumps mean you may have used **too much liquid** or a **combination of liquid and salts**. Ensure you are measuring each and every batch to the suggested measurements.

Resources & Suppliers

Anya's at Planktown Hardware & More
www.planktownhardware.com
8117 Planktown North Rd
Shiloh, OH 44878
1-419-896-3581

Bramble Berry
http://www.brambleberry.com
info@brambleberry.com
1-877-627-7883
Dry ingredients, molds, and scents

Elements Bath and Body
http://www.elementsbathandbody.com
502-690-2520
8851 Lagrange Road
Smithfield, KY 40068
Fragrances, dry ingredients molds

Majestic Mountain Sage
http://www.thesage.com
info@thesage.com
1-435-755-0863
Soap and cosmetic making supplies

Rustic Escentuals
http://RusticEscentuals.com
TechSupport@RusticEscentuals.com
1-864-582-9335
1050 Canaan Road
Roebuck, SC 29376
Bath bomb molds, scents, micas

Soap Equipment
http://www.soapequipment.com
Bath Bomb Machines and Equipment
Shrink-wrap systems

Wholesale Supplies Plus
http://www.wholesalesuppliesplus.com
10035 Broadview Road
Broadview Heights, Ohio 44147
Contact@WholesaleSuppliesPlus.com
1-800-359-0944
* Bath Bomb Ball Mold – 2.75", shown on page 8.

Contributors & Testers

Michelle Arce
Made with Lots of Love, LLC
http://www.madewithlotsoflove.com

Angela Carillo
Alegna Soap
http://www.alegnasoap.com

Debbie Lusetti Bruijn
Fairhope Soap Company
http://www.fairhopesoapcompany.com

Amanda Griffin
lovinsoap.com / lovinsoapproject.org

Tricia Samundssen
Scentability
http://www.scentability.net

T.A Stewart Helton
Coffee house Suds
http://www.etsy.com/shop/coffeehouse
suds

Charlene M Simon
Bathhouse Soapery & Caldarium
www.bathhousesoap.com

Stephanie Weaver Thompson
WaxWorx Custom Candles, llc
http://www.waxworxcandles.com/

Tanya Rasley
Baby Duck Soap Co.
http://www.babyducksoap.com

Acknowledgements

To the lord my God, for allowing me to do what I love.

To my mom for all of her encouragement and love.

To Hollie, my best friend for being a life giver and always having my back and supporting me.

To my wonderful sons, Cody and Josh, for being my constant inspiration and motivation.

To my Momma Anne for always believing in me.

To Amanda, my soapy sister for always pushing me to do great things and inspiring me.

To my sweet friends, Kirin, Gaytrice, Angie, Niki, Theresa, and Stephanie for their support and inspiration.

To my wonderful editor, Stephanie Orange, for making this process such an enjoyable one.

To Michelle Klohe for the help and inspiration with the name of this book.

To all my soapy peeps that encourage me on a daily basis.

To Kayla Fioravanti for inspiring me to write this book.

To Marla Bosworth, for encouraging be to go outside my box.

To Debbie May, Debbie Chialtas and Anne-Marie Faiola for inspiring me to start this business.

To all my amazing followers and their constant support of my soapy business.

To my friend Cheryl, for going on a Yule log hunt with me on a snowy winters day.

To Nina for her impromptu and unexpected, but much appreciated proofreading.

To all of you who have encouraged me along the way asking questions, sending pictures of failed attempts and successes. This book would not have been made with out you!

There are so many more I wished I could list, but *you know who you are*!

I saved the best for last.

To my husband, Chris, my supporter, my encourager, my assistant, my F-BOMBER (aka Fizzy Bomber).

Thank you for supporting me and letting me do what I love.

Thank you for always being my right hand in this soapy adventure.

Happy 20th Anniversary!

About the Author

Holly Port is the owner of Lotion Bar Cafe (**www.lotionbarcafe.com**) in Colorado Springs, Colorado. She is a wife of 20 years, mother of two teenage sons, soapmaker, teacher, and author. Since 2006 she has been making soaps, bath fizzies, lip balms, and of course, lotion bars. Her soaping motto is "Every Bar Has a Story...." because each bar is very personal and from the heart.

Since the beginning of her business she has donated to a care point in Swaziland, Africa through an organization called Beyond Survival that works to provide opportunity for people to live beyond basic survival, whether it be educationally, spiritually, financially and medically.

Each year she also hosts her own "Handmade *Holly*day" craft show from her home in Colorado Springs, CO, that showcases other local women artists. She is very passionate and encouraging to helping others' build their businesses.

In 2013 she began a relationship with Harvest Home, located in Missouri. Holly mentors a group of woman by teaching them soapmaking as a new skill. This skill will help support the women through the healing steps from their abuse.

In January she joined the Lovin' Soap Project Collaborative and has been sharing her knowledge in the monthly publication, which aims to empower women in other countries.

She believes **one person can make a difference**.

Professionally Holly is certified in Cold Process Soap Making from the HSCG. She enjoys traveling and teaching classes across the country and makes the most of every moment. She enjoys selling at farmers markets, local craft shows and to stores and she also is a member of the Handcrafted Soap and Cosmetic Guild.

www.lotionbarcafe.com - Wholesale/Retail

www.beyondsurvival.org
www.harvesthome.org

www.lovinsoapproject.com
www.soapguild.org

A fizzy a day will take all your
stresses away!

Illustration by Tracey Sims Gurley

Made in the USA
San Bernardino, CA
01 May 2017